Poetry Loves Most Beautiful

Poetry Loves Most Beautiful

Viktor Sandalj

RESOURCE *Publications* · Eugene, Oregon

POETRY LOVES MOST BEAUTIFUL

Resource Publications
An Imprint of Wipf and Stock Publishers
199 W. 8th Ave., Suite 3
Eugene, OR 97401

www.wipfandstock.com

PAPERBACK ISBN: 978-1-6667-7263-0
HARDCOVER ISBN: 978-1-6667-7264-7
EBOOK ISBN: 978-1-6667-7265-4

04/20/23

Contents

Listen To Your Guardian Angel's Pray

You have no idea how much a heart can love.
Even less how much it can hurt.
Don't let it hit rock bottom.
Don't let it eat dirt.

Whenever you're down and low,
Listen to your guardian angel's pray.
You'll come out a winner!
Saying "What a wonderful day".

In the Name of Sanity

You are always by my side, always next to me,
Purging through the edge of sanity.

You are always way too kind, your love is hard to find,
With eyes I'm completely blind, with you the last thing
on my mind.

You are always in my mind, even in my dreams,
When you are in pain, I can hear your screams.

I Forgave Her—She Loved Me

I forgave her, she loved me.
She was true, she never lied to me.
She let me be me.
Then she left me.

Here comes the rain,
Here comes the pain,
Here comes the fact,
That drives me insane,
Her love is gone and
I'll never see her again.

Here comes the pain, that's so different from the rest.
Here comes the pain, that'll put your mind to the test.
Here comes the horror, of not knowing tomorrow.
Here comes the weight, of the burdens of sorrow.

Eyes full of pain.
Pouring bloody rain.
All hope gone in vain.
Overkill insane.

When Your World Feels Unreal

What do you do,
If you can't find the peace of mind?
What do you do,
If the world's unkind?

What do you think,
If you head isn't in sync?
What do you think,
If you can't even blink?

What do you feel,
If they make you squeal?
What do you feel,
If this world feels unreal?

What do you see,
If you disagree?
What do you see,
If they make you flee?

What do you sense,
If there's no evidence?
What do you sense,
When you just can't make no sense?

Science of the Mind

They'll convince you you're unwell.
They'll tell you your life is hell.
We'll just do another test.
Let's hope for the best.

They'll tell you it's all a lie.
They'll make you fucking cry.
You just have to take these pills.
And you will never feel these numbing chills.

They'll tell you just another try.
They'll find all the reason why.
Just take these six a day.
To make your demons go away.

They'll tell you, you have no friends.
They'll tell you your life ends.
You just need to make amends.
And take these pills—these special blends.

Will you ever find,
That peace of mind?
Please be so kind
To silence your fucking mind.

They'll tell you to bow down.
They'll make you their own clown.
We now know you're better.
To us you really matter.

They'll tell you that they care.
They'll tell you life's unfair.
But you know you'll recover.
Or they will just put you under.

They'll tell you: you aren't the first.
They will surely quench your thrust.
You just need something stronger.
Coz without them you can live no longer.

They'll make you completely blind.
They'll silence all your mind.
Telling you, you're one of a kind.
Careful, so you're not the one they find.

Will you ever find,
That peace of mind?
Please be so kind to,
Silence your mind.

Mirror, Mirror

Mirror, mirror on the wall,
Who will catch me when I fall?
Who will tell me where to crawl?
Translate these writings on the wall.

Who will pick up when I call?
Who will make me feel so small?
Who will make my heart crumble?
In this mirror, who is it so very humble?

Leaving Here

Sick of all the lies,
Phony smiles and harsh goodbyes.
Stunned, yet time flies,
In harmony with these wicked lies.

When will it stop?
Will I move on from here?
Will I meet someone,
Without feeling fear?

So close is the time,
That I'll just up and leave,
The best thing to do,
Last thing up my sleeve.

Enough is enough,
Too much Déjà vu.
Meeting you here,
For the last fuck-you.

Will it ever change?
All this doom and gloom.
Time to re-arrange,
The colourful costume.

Kindness is a Thing or Two

Kindness is a thing or two,
A language spoken by a few.
Never close your heart, never shut its gate.
Shout it out loud, before it's too late.

Another morning comes, and you've got no one to love.
Open the windows and wait for your dove.
Do not die alone. Call her on the phone.
Maybe the time has passed, but make the kindness a feeling to last.

Royal Chill

Cold winter royal,
Put my hear on trial,
Passion gone, death desire.

You're this polar princess,
A cold heart witness,
With no other interest.

Plane queen of cold,
You spit words out,
No thought—just fannying about.

With this freeze,
And nothing in between.
You lead me, to the life of sin.

On top of your cold throne,
Your eyes send the chills,
While your mind plainly kills.

Where others look,
Is not known.
In your eyes, they will be overthrown.

Just in time,
To see my heart squeeze.
Stopwatch—freeze.

In her soul,
Completely no control.
The cold feels cold.

The atoms of love,
You'll manage,
To freeze.

Flawless Love Song

I'm hard wired to your heart,
I think it will explode,
All my feelings running wild,
Madness overload.

Baby, you hit me hard,
Right from the very start.
Big collision,
Yet, nothing fell apart!

Every time to see your smile,
I'll run for you an extra mile.
You're a girl with class and style,
In my mind you have a special file.

You bring me luck like a four leaf clover
You have a halo floating over.
When I kiss you, kiss me slower,
I wanna do it over and over.

Only you I see in this city,
So smart, so witty, so cute, so pretty.
I love the power of your brain,
It positively drives me insane.

You're a girl so unique,
Meeting you I've reach my peek.
You put me on a winning streak,
My heart is yours, take it quick!

I know my life you'll prolong,
So, I write you this love song.
With you I won't live the life of sin,
Baby we will live to win.

A new love born,
I'm electrified,
From your contact,
My old self died.

When we touch, I restart,
You're more than a sweet, sweet-heart.
Great collision,
Yet nothing fell apart.

I'm hard wired to your heart,
I think it will explode.
When you aren't in my mind,
It will just implode.

New One

This new lady I've met,
Radiates positively with optimism.
And the kind hope raises,
Overall enthusiasm.

I starred in awe and wouldn't let,
This moment pass,
So very soon,
She is brighter than the sun on the moon.

She is caring, kind,
Most loving.
I smile as I see,
What this moment's becoming.

The beautiful lady,
Has most wonderful eyes.
That have a look,
To stun as time flies.

In perfect time we've met,
As I see we both need a change.
Let it be . . .
Let the stars dust re-arrange.

My heart is finally set,
To love or not at all.
To give her all,
Or completely lose control.

By first look,
I cannot say one bad word.
But humbly ask her,
Will you be my world?

Those Eyes That I See

Whenever I close my eyes,
I see your pretty face.
Looking down on me,
Filling the empty space.

I can always see you pretty eyes,
Warmer than the sun.
I would always watch them,
Rather than anyone.

Those eyes that I see,
Bring joy and peace to me.
Tears of joy just flow,
So, I can't wait to see them again tomorrow.

From shear nothingness,
You bring a smile to my face.
A smile so bright,
Brighter than the morning light.

And all I wanna see,
Is only you and me.
And only with you,
I ever wanna be.

I Want You

I want you in my bed,
I want you in my arms,
I want to give you
All my lucky charms.

I want you in my sleep,
I want you in my eyes,
I want you alive,
As this flash flies.

I want you in my blood,
I want you in my veins,
I want you thunder,
Deep inside my brains.

I want you so close,
I want to be the one,
I want to be your only friend,
Your only sun.

Your Beauty Lights Up the Night

I'm gonna shout,
All right!
Your beauty glows,
Into the night!

I'm gonna shout
It's alight!
I wanna hold you,
So tight.

I wanna shout,
You're mine!
With you,
I walk down the line.

I wanna shout,
It's alright!
I kiss you,
Goodnight.

Thunder In My Heart

Thunder in my heart, is louder than the sun,
If I don't know you, I don't know anyone.

Such a gleaming beauty, who wouldn't say she loves me,
She never said the words, that could really renew me.

If she could say, that one line verse,
She would have opened up, a whole new universe.

I Picked My Star in the Universe

Pick the brightest star.

It's you.

Pick the shiniest start.

It's you.

Pick the largest star.

It's you.

Pick my favourite star.

It's you.

Pick the best star.

It's you.

Pick the most loving star.

It's you.

You Will Never Cry Again

You'll feel when it's time,
You'll know when.
To be by my side,
You'll never cry again.

The sky is crying, when you're sad,
The earth's shaking, when you're mad.
One wrong though, all gone bad.
She's the best thing I ever had.

Parting Time

What leads me further away,
Is time to say goodbye.
It's piercing my heart,
When it's nearby.

I always want you close,
Right in my arms,
I never wanna feel,
When parting time comes.

In Time—PART I

Hottest, most gentle woman,
That I have ever seen,
For such creation,
Millions of years in between.

She will give me kindness,
And all the love I need,
She will kiss me softly,
Set my heart at lightning speed.

All I need is you love,
To get me through the night,
All my eyes are seeing,
Is you in the light.

More and more is coming,
Of feelings overload,
If I do not share them,
My heart will explode.

A nice quiet life,
Is all that I need,
With you together,
This life I wanna lead.

Be by my side,
Forever and ever and ever,
And I will love you darling
From now until forever.

All I need is more,
To start to feel alright,
All my soul can feel,
Is your soul's special light.

In Time—PART II

I wish you were with me,
To share the warmth of the bed.
To feel the real you,
Not a flame in my head.

Someone to cuddle,
Late into the night,
Someone to kiss,
To make me feel all right.

I wish to see you once more,
On a beautiful island we met.
Because if I don't ask you,
That's something I'll regret.

I've met a perfect,
Most wonderful woman for me.
I also hope that she accept,
The most beautiful mermaid to be.

Rags to riches,
As the saying goes,
When you're with me,
Everything just flows.

Someone to cuddle,

Close to a fire place,

To keep you very warm,

And see the beauty of your face.

Just one more sentence,

To complete the thoughts in my mind,

You are so special,

A diamond one of a kind.

Your Beautiful Eyes Enlighten Me

You've got most beautiful blue eyes,

I hope they never tell me any lies,

When I look at them everything's still,

Yet the time flies,

When I look at them I see a pacifier,

Before dawn they're my appetizer,

They look at me with such kindness,

They're perfect example of a path to rightness,

I wish I see them every morning and last thing at night,

Even when there's darkness I can see their special light,

They look at me and brake all the chains,

Blood is pumping fast through my veins,

They set my heart in flames,

And they know at what my heart aims,

To kiss you and take you to new domains.

The Woman I've Found

Can I say I found a woman for myself?
Can I say I didn't wanna meet anybody else?
Can I say that with her I'm truly happy?
I feel her love, no more, no less.

Can I say that she's the one for me?
If I ask her, she will agree.
Can I take her for a long, long walk?
So, she giggles when we talk.

Can she be the tangible one?
Shining brighter than the morning sun.
She's the kindest person I've been around,
I'm truly happy with the love I've found.

Doating

Gleaming from above,
Is your doating love,
For me.

Written in the starts,
Is the path,
For a brand-new start.

Carved start dust,
Is the way,
It should have been.

Deeper that the ocean
Is my magic potion,
You clear blue eyes.

High up in the skies
Spelled in the clouds
Words that ring:

I love you.

Fill me up with Kindness

Emptiness in me,
You've filled up with your eyes.
With you resetting me,
My feeling never dies.

My lonely heart,
You've shown the way.
A marvelous feeling,
When your mind doesn't wonder astray.

I can't see anything but your lightning goodness.
You shall bring me some dear greatness.
You are a path to success.
You fill in my emptiness.

All paths lead to you.
Darling, I love you!

Midnight Flower

Midnight flower,
Blooming by the well.
She needs to be wild,
Not held up in a cell.

During the day,
She rests till crack of dawn.
To everyone she seems,
Like a pitch black swan.

She needs to be free,
Like a blooming red rose.
Everything withers,
Whenever away she goes.

Kissing her softly,
Is a perfect crime.
Cherry flavored,
That's how she likes her rhyme.

A dragon like lady,
A little fiery, maybe?
All I truly know,
She drives me positively fucking crazy.

All I want is more,
Of her alluring smell.
New life has grown,
Where her leaf fell.

From This

Look at me,
What do you see,
Darkness.

Look at me,
What do you feel,
Surreal.

Look at me,
What do you sense,
Total menace.

Look at me,
Where will I go,
I just don't know.

Look at me,
I'm wired,
From this shit retired.

Quick Hello—Fast Goodbye

I promise you miracle days,
I want us together to go on about our ways,
I promise you hearts and flowers,
I want us together for hours and hours.

I want to be your one and only,
I want you to see I respect all the love that you gave,
I want to be the one you call,
I don't ever wanna see you fall.

Purple Sun

You're like the ace of spades,
Only one that shines as this country fades.

You're like the ace of red,
If I ain't with you I'm as good as dead.

You're like the real time lover,
Don't take crap from any motherfucker.

You're like a flower is spring,
Only the best in me you bring.

You're my purple sun,
If you don't shine, I see no one.

Do You Know?

Do you know how much I love you?

Do you know how much I care?

Do you know how much I adore you?

Do you know how much I wanna hold your hand?

Do you know how much I wanna kiss you?

Do you know how much I miss you?

Do you know how much you mean to me?

Do you know how much I wanna be your man?

Do you know how much I love you?

Do you know how much I care?

Do you know how much I think of you?

Do you know what I'd do, if you aren't there.

Please Accept My Heart's Light

Love me tonight,
Love me all night.
Generously accept,
My heart's light.

Love me more,
Love me the most.
Love me above all,
No matter what the cost.

Love me deeply,
Love me tenderly.
Give this heart,
A good medley.

Love me good.
Love me better.
Love me best.
Forget about the rest.

Nothing Will Let You Down

I want to write you a song,
Because I haven't seen you in way too long.
How great is it to hear,
Your whisper in my ear.

In a rocky country,
From the island you left behind.
With wonderful memories,
Imprinted in your mind.

In this world of constant hurry,
Just stay yourself and keep calm.
Also stay beautiful and honest,
And nothing will let you down.

Many great memories,
Are sure to come.
Just keep believing,
In the person you've become.

Never let them,
Exploit the real you.
Staying honest to yourself,
Is the best thing you can do.

Has She Lost Her Way

If I keep talking to you,
Something might change.
Your heart, your thoughts,
Might re-arrange.

I keep attempting,
For the sake of it.
Yet my every attempt,
You deliberately forsake it.

Too much pride,
Is your little blonde mind.
I crawl to you,
Yet you're so unkind.

You never cared,
For a thing I say.
Are you just another girl,
Who lost her way?

Kindest Face and Warmest Smile

Have you ever loved anyone,
More than life itself?
Have you ever lost control,
When she told you she loves you herself?

Have you ever been in love,
So deeply you can't decide,
That her initials,
In your heart you want to inscribe?

Have you ever felt nothing,
But kindness your way?
Have you ever been left with your mouth open,
With not a word to say?

If you ever had, don't be scared,
To ask her to with you, share her life.
Get down on one knee,
Open the ring box and ask her to be your wife.

Check Mate

I love this game we play,
How I'm courting you.
You smile and send me kisses,
The way you want me to.

I love when we run on the sand,
At the peak of dawn.
I'm right behind you,
Trying to catch on.

I love the late-night dinners,
By the candle in the night.
Your beauty glows,
Brighter than the light.

I love the coffee you make,
Served with a kiss.
Nothing is so sweet,
Not like this.

I love all the time with you,
As it feels all right.
You by my side,
Is the only thing that's right.

Maybe

Maybe if I'm the last man standing,
You will love me.

Maybe if there's no one else.
You will love me.

Maybe I am the last man standing.
You shall know, but I don't know when.

I am your man.
Take me.
Then.

This Fuckin' Ace of Spades

This ace, this ace,
She's all but full of grace.

This maze, this maze,
Her mind infiltrated with sickening rays.

Her face, her face,
All but of human race.

This race, this race,
Deranged all over the place.

This chase, this chase,
Through a matrix with no arrays.

Her phase, her phase,
Another fucking mindless disgrace.

This ace, this ace,
Running all over the fucking place.

This night, this night,
It's gonna be alright.

Once Upon a Time in an Unloved Heart

An evil eye looks upon you,

Thinking what she will put you through.

A dark woman with an evil soul,

She's mistaken thinking she's in control.

An evil woman with mysterious treachery,

Will finish you off later, maybe.

A ghost in one horse town,

With a smirk build her private clown.

A back darkness downed upon me,

I always come back, could never be free.

With loaded tricks up her sleeves,

A notorious net for me she weaves.

Time will come when you will pay,

In hell, have a nice day.

The Future is Bright

All this time,
I had conjured dreams about you.
Now that you appeared,
I don't know what to do.

What exactly have I needed you for?
Now, that you're looking at me in this real world.
I dig deep in my mind,
For such love is hard to find.

Time has come,
Time is bright.
Future is clear,
Future is bright.
I have someone to kiss goodnight.

Leave everything behind.
You've come to me,
A unique kind.

Why just now,
After all this time?
With you I'll do,
Some over time.

You make me feel,
Like a neuron start.
My mind is clear,
With a mental scar.

All you do,
Is dream of me.
My heart's breathing,
My shackles are free.

All this time,
I felt you'd come.
From another time,
From another realm.

Never leave me,
Nor my side,
You've come out,
Of my beautiful mind.

I fell in love with a lady,
So beautiful, mesmerizing and kind.
She's the only thing that's right,
In my beautiful mind.

I Dream of Angels Tonight

I dream of angels tonight.
I hope you do too.
I hope you hear their melody,
To the words "I love you".

I dream of angles tonight.
I can see one too, it is you.
Telling me some soothing words:
"Darling, I love you."